to dearest Leslie

From Cornwall
With Love

and from myself also —

Jacky.

x

January 2000.

From Cornwall
With Love

An evocative view of Cornwall photographed by BOB CROXFORD

We go to Cornwall on Thursday. That is the beginning.

Published by ATMOSPHERE

To Jenny & Becky.
For their patience

FROM CORNWALL WITH LOVE

Photographs Copyright Bob Croxford 1993
Text copyright Bob Croxford 1993
(Except where separately acknowledged)
Anthology compilation copyright Bob Croxford

Design copyright Ann Butcher and Atmosphere.

Third Impression 1998

First published by ATMOSPHERE in 1993
Atmosphere Publishing
Willis Vean
Mullion
Helston Cornwall TR12 7DF
TEL : 01326-240180
FAX : 01326-240900

ISBN 0-9521850-0-8

Designed by Ann Butcher
Origination by Scantec Repro, Cornwall
Printed and bound in Italy by L.E.G.O. Vicenza

COVER PICTURE: South Cornwall Coastline
BACKGROUND: Beach Pebbles

Also by Bob Croxford

FROM DEVON WITH LOVE *ISBN 0 9521850 1 6*

FROM BATH WITH LOVE *ISBN 0-9521850-2-4*

FROM THE COTSWOLDS WITH LOVE *ISBN 0-9521850-4-0*

FROM DORSET WITH LOVE *ISBN 0-9521850-3-2*

CONTENTS

INTRODUCTION

I first arrived in Cornwall many years ago. Then, it was a place largely untouched by the drastic changes which had occurred in the rest of the country. Each town and village had a different character. There were few major new roads and the local economy was more viable than at present.

So-called modern improvements now occur almost every day. Many of these changes are caused by pressures outside the traditional economy. Modern roads bring supermarkets which decimate the local shops. This is blurring differences across the country. An alien motif is making itself felt.

But Cornwall is a rugged place. The pounding waves of the Atlantic fashioned her coastline. The character of the Cornish landscape was shaped by the weather. On this rugged anvil the character of the people was wrought. People who in turn built strong stone hedges, granite harbour walls and some awesome holes in the ground.

The life in Cornish towns and villages has always been at the edge of economic decline. Apart from a brief period, when the county was the world centre for tin mining, there has been little prosperity here. When the tin mining declined, the money and riches went with the up-country speculators. Even the industrial revolution, which started in Cornwall, moved to be nearer the Midland coal-fields.

There are still many magic parts of Cornwall which are unchanged. Places one can go to recharge ones batteries.

The other evening, I went to a spot on the clifftops in North Cornwall. Between heavy showers, I struggled down slippery wet grass and up over rocky outcrops. I set up my camera on a tripod and, with great difficulty, in the howling wind, changed to an appropriate lens. Several times the tripod and case were nearly blown over the cliffs. The sun was just setting into a bank of tumultuous clouds. I made a few exposures, and then looked around. As the light faded I sat in the shelter of a stone hedge. The view was magnificent. It had a wild Cornish quality, the atmosphere was indefinable. It was the stuff of books, poetry and drama. The wind hammered the sea to a flat metaled mirror reflecting the dying sunlight. The light in the sky was golden, but the glow was cool, as it bathed the foreground with its fading strength. The scene was truly memorable, but, I was the only witness.

Perhaps I photograph the world through rose tinted spectacles. I see things in the landscape which many others do not. By choosing times of day and seasons when no one else is there I see light and drama all around.

In this book I have not tried to be comprehensive. I have attempted to show my view of the landscapes, seascapes, towns, harbours and villages. My view is a romantic one. I have not shown the dark side except as a gentle counterpoint to the beauty which abounds in Cornwall. I appreciate that many others would see the place differently.

This collection of photographs is not a guide or catalogue. No single picture will show all there is of the place. Hopefully this selection, taken together, will make up the jigsaw that is the Cornish landscape.

This is a book of landscape pictures. I am not a people photographer. However, I am often aware that people have shaped the landscape.

The text which accompanies the photographs is an anthology of Cornish writing, past and present. Some of the writing for various reasons strikes a chord with my own feelings. Derek Tangye's description of a night arrival reminds me of my own arrival in Cornwall during a lush summer's moonlit night. And many times I have stood alone, with a camera, while observing an early dawn or dramatic sunset, and had the same thoughts as Kenneth Grahame's mole; 'Oh my! Oh my! Oh my!.'

I have often thought that writers encapsulate my own feelings about the sense of place more than other photographers. The landscape has an affect on everyone but some convey that feeling with better fluency. In the selection of the quotes I have chosen some for period quaintness and some for humour.

The style of writing varies with time. The coming of the railways brought a spate of books which were no more than a fortnight of holiday memories. In a few instances these books have a frisson of interest because of changes since their first publication. Dinah Craik's amazingly sentimental 'Unsentimental Journey Through Cornwall' from 1884 is full of contrasts with the present day.

A few writers like Charles Dickens and Arthur Conan Doyle wrote too little of their journeys to Cornwall but what they wrote shows the effect the county had.

Some writers came to Cornwall with great enthusiasm. D H Lawrence, who arrived with great hopes for a new life, was eventually expelled by the police. They believed he, and his wife, were spies during the Great War. George Bernard Shaw who feigned indifference before his first trip, was later to be much more enthusiastic. He started writing 'The Doctor's Dilemma' on the beach at Mevagissey. The third act was written on St. Austell railway station, while waiting for a train. It is not recorded how fast he wrote or how late the train was!

In more recent times the writing changed. Resident writers like C C Vyvyan, Denys Val Baker and Sven Berlin bring true creativity to their work. The visitors too like Paul Theroux and Mark Wallington, have become more imaginative and have original viewpoints.

This selection of writing is not intended to act as captions or commentary for the photographs and should not be thought of in conjunction with the images. Instead it expresses an alternative view. Taken together, the words too, make a sense of the place that is Cornwall.

But remember, in Denys Val Baker's words;

'…in a timeless land which still belongs remarkably to the shadows of the past, of other worlds, the only possible answers must be intangible. If Cornwall could be explained, it would cease to be Cornwall.'

Cornish traditions are very contradictory. On the one hand we have amid the rocks and the hills numerous devil's coits, plenty of devil's footsteps, with devil's bellows, devil's frying pans, devil's ovens and devil's caves in abundance. On the other hand we are told that the devil never came to Cornwall, 'because when he crossed the Tamar, and made Torpoint for a brief space his resting place, he could not but observe that everything vegetable or animal was put by Cornish people into a pie. He saw and heard of fishy pie, star-gazy pie, conger pie, and, indeed, pies of all the fishes of the sea; of parsley pie, and herby pie, of lamy pie, and pies without number. Therefore, fearing they might take a fancy to a devilly pie, he took himself back into Devonshire.'

ROBERT HUNT

Pisky fine, pisky gay!
Pisky now will fly away.

Pisky new coat, and pisky new hood,
Pisky now will do no more good.

ANON

< Cornish Piskie

Cornish Pasty >

......where headland after headland flamed far into the rich heart of the west.

ALFRED LORD TENNYSON

Pistol : what is thy name?
King Henry : (in disguise as a common soldier): Harry Le Roy.
Pistol : Le Roy! a Cornish name: art thou of Cornish crew?

WILLIAM SHAKESPEARE

When I set out for Lyonnesse,
A hundred miles away,
The rime was on the spray,
And starlight lit my lonesomeness
When I set out for Lyonnesse
A Hundred miles away.

THOMAS HARDY

Bude Beach Sunset >

< Beach Chalets

Artists and tourists haunt this picturesque nook. A village built at the end of a deep narrow creek, which runs far inland, and is a safe shelter for vessels of considerable size. On either side is a high footpath, leading to two headlands, from both of which the views of the sea and coast are very fine. And there are relics of antiquity and legends thereto belonging - a green mound, all that remains of Bottrieux Castle; and Ferrabury Church, with its silent tower. A peal of bells had been brought, and the ship which carried them had nearly reached the cove, when the pilot, bidding the captain "thank God for his safe voyage," was answered that he "thanked only himself and a fair wind." Immediately a storm arose; and the ship went down with every soul on board - except the pilot. So the church tower is mute - but on winter nights the lost bells are still heard, sounding mournfully from the depths of the sea.

DINAH MULOCH CRAIK

Boscastle Fishing Boat >

< Boscastle Harbour

*S*uch a trip as we had into Cornwall...... If you could have followed us into the earthy old churches and into the strange caverns of the gloomy seashore, and down into the depths of mines, and up to the top of giddy heights where unspeakable green water was roaring. If you could have seen but one gleam of the bright fires by which we sat in the big rooms of ancient inns at night, until long after the small hours had come and gone, or smelt but one steam of hot punch which came in every evening in a huge broad china bowl. I never laughed so much in my life as I did in this journey.

CHARLES DICKENS

Rocky Valley Maze >

< Old Post Office, Tintagel

*B*y Tre, Pol and Pen shall ye know Cornishmen.

R S HAWKER

*T*he Rain it Raineth Every Day

NORMAN GARSTIN

< Port Isaac Rooftops

Port Isaac >

*Now, we were entering surfing country proper. Everywhere
were signs advertising boards for hire and all along Watergate
Bay surfers sat in the water in their black wetsuits; from the clifftop
they looked like flies on a pane of glass.*

MARK WALLINGTON

We used to picnic where the thrift
Grew deep and tufted to the edge;
We saw the yellow foam-flakes drift
In trembling sponges on the ledge
Below us, till the wind would lift
Them up the cliff and o'er the hedge.
Sand in the sandwiches, wasps in the tea,
Sun on our bathing-dresses heavy with the wet,
Squelch of the bladder-wrack waiting for the sea,
Fleas round the tamarisk, an early cigarette.

JOHN BETJEMAN

< Bucket and Spade

Polzeath Sunset >

*T*he washerwoman who has part of the double cottage along the lane says that she would go mad if she went to live in a town, and that the mere thought of it, sometimes, as she goes in and out of her door all day long, makes her feel uneasy.

The miller says that the people do not notice the beauty of the place much, because they are used to it; but he himself told me that, so far as he can hear, it is the prettiest place in England.

ARTHUR SYMONS

From Pentire Point to Lundy Light
Is a watery grave by day or night

R S HAWKER

Padstow Mayday >

< Padstow Harbour at Dusk

*T*he Loneliness of Cornwall is a loneliness unchanged by the presence of men, its freedoms a freedom inexpressible by description or epitaph. You cannot say Cornwall is this, or that. You cannot describe it in a word or visualise it in a second. You may know the country from east to west and sea to sea, but if you close your eyes and think about it no clear-cut image rises before you. In this quality of changefulness have we possibly surprised the secret of Cornwall's wild spirit - in this intimacy the essence of its charm? Cornwall!

C C VYVYAN

*H*ow I wish you were here - as only the Cornish see its stupendous merits.

VIRGINIA WOOLF

< Porthcothan Beach

Porthcothan Spring Flowers >

*Suddenly, as if some enchanter had
waved his wand, the mist lifted and
a blaze of sunshine gilded the
splendid coastline and crested, with
rainbow hues, the great waves. The
tide was on the turn and, here and
there, were patches of golden sand
broken up by black rocks. I felt I
must shout, sing or do something to
hail such a majestic beauty.*

*A*nd on the sounding soft funereal shore
   They, watching till the days should wholly die,
Saw the far sea sweep to the far grey sky,
Saw the long sands sweep to the long grey sea.
And night made one sweet mist of moor and lea,
And only far off shore the foam gave light,
And life in them sank silent as the night.

< Bedruthan from the Air

Bedruthan Steps >

I remember feeling a deep indefinable satisfaction, even when I was quite small, whenever I was taken on to a beach and could watch the waves sliding in over the shingle. The Cornish seas were much more exciting than the refined Sunny South Coast variety.

NOEL COWARD

Day breaks o'er Cornwall's Celtic ground
And tints the landscape wide around
With many a varied dye.

SIR JAMES BROOKE

< Holywell Cave

Newquay Harbour >

26

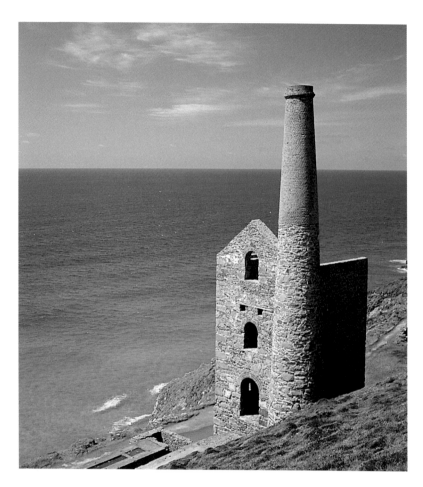

Now we will speak something of the tin that is dug and gotten there. They that inhabit the British promontory Balerium, by reason of their converse with merchants, are more civilised and courteous to strangers than the rest are. These are the people that make the tin, which with a great deal of care and labour they dig out of the ground; and that being rocky, the metal is mixed with some veins of earth, out of which they melt the metal, and then refine it; then they beat it into four-square pieces like a dye, and carry it to a British isle near at hand, called Ictis. For at low tide, all being dry between them and the island, they convey over in carts abundance of tin in the meantime. But there is one peculiar to these islands which lie between Britain and Europe; for at full sea they appear to be islands, but at low water for a long way they look like so many peninsulas. Hence the merchants transport the tin they buy of the inhabitants to France; and for thirty days journey they carry it in packs upon horse backs through France to the mouth of the river Rhone.

DIODORUS SICULUS 1ST CENT. BC

< *Wheal Coates*

Wheal Coates Sunset >

St Jes is two miles or more from Lannant. The place that the chief of the Toun hath and partly dooth satande yn is a very peninsula, and is extendid into the Sea of Severn as a Cape. Most Part of the Houses in the Peninsula be sore oppressid or overcoverid with Sandes that the stormy Windes and Rages castith up ther; this Calamite hath continuid ther little above 20 yeres. The best part of the Toun now standith in the South Part of the Peninsula, up towards another Hille, for Defence from the Sandes. There is a Blok House and a fair Pere in the Est side of the Peninsula, but the Pere is sore chokid with Sande. The Poroch Chirch is a Ja, a noble Man's Daughter of Ireland and Disciple of S Barricus.

JOHN LELAND

The Vicar of St. Ives says the smell of fish there is sometimes so terrific as to stop the church clock.

FRANCIS KILVERT

Godrevy Lighthouse >

< St. Ives

O spring has set off her green fuses
Down by the Tamar today,
And careless, like tidemarks, the hedges
Are bursting with almond and may.

Here lie I, waiting for old summer,
A red face and straw-coloured hair has he:
I shall meet him on the road from Marazion
And the Mediterranean Sea.

September has flung a spray of rooks
On the sea-chart of the sky,
The tall shipmasts crack in the forest
And the banners of autumn fly.

My room is a bright glass cabin,
All Cornwall thunders at my door,
And the white ships of winter lie
In the sea-roads of the moor.

CHARLES CAUSLEY

< Zennor

Cape Cornwall >

32

*T*he Cornish drolls are dead, each one;
　　The fairies from their haunts have gone.
There's scarce a witch in all the land,
The world has grown so learn'd and grand.

HENRY QUICK

*A*t the Mên-an-Tol there is supposed to be a guardian fairy or
pixy who can make miraculous cures. And my mother knew of
an actual case in which a changeling was put through the stone in
order to get the real child back. It seems that evil pixies changed
children, and that the pixy at Mên-an Tol being good, in opposition,
undo their work.

QUOTED BY W Y EVANS WENTZ

< Roadside Cross

Mên-an-Tol >

I am living now in a little wooden house on the highest part of the moor that separates the two seas, north and south between Zennor and Penzance. All round, on all sides, nothing but open moorland and rock-strewn hills, mostly crowned with marvelous Druidic temples. Without leaving the house I can see the sun rise at five in the morning, and watch it sink at night into the sea. The sky never grows dark; the darkness seems rather to come welling out of the earth like a dye, in using into every shape and form, every twig and every stone, keen, intense blackness...

PETER WARLOCK

*T*he open coliseum of each little cove of sand or rock may be the theatre for any natural, supernatural or unnatural event. The unending presence of the sea breathing ceaselessly over the shoulder of each hill, the rock charged with a thousand sunsets or carved by a hundred years of rain, the little trees loaded with berries growing away from the prevailing wind, offering crimson to green, the mind's incessant vertigo at the cliff edge, and the slow constructional flight of the seagull - these things in some way act as the charming of magicians and open up the deeper rooms of experience in man, making him aware of his being part of the natural universe, at the head of a great unseen procession of gods, and devils, spectres and dragons; of being a channel for unknown and undefined forces; of facing the mystery of life, awakening powers of perception which search beyond the frontiers of normal events.

SVEN BERLIN

< Sennen

Botallack >

For me the seas and the moors and skies and rocks of Cornwall are inexhaustible material. Then always there's this peculiar clarity of light, throwing the landscape of West Penwith into perspective. It's a land of great antiquity, primeval, sometimes savage - why even on a hot day the skies still hold threats of storm clouds...

DENYS VAL BAKER

The startled waves leap over it; the storm
Smites it with all the scourges of the rain,
And steadily against its solid form
Press the great shoulders of the hurricane.

LONGFELLOW

< Penberth

Land's End >

Indeed, along this Cornish coast, life and death seem very near together. Every pleasure carries with it a certain amount of risk; the utmost caution is required both on land and sea, and I cannot advise either rash or nervous people to go travelling in Cornwall.

DINAH MULOCH CRAIK

....really the loveliest village in England.

DYLAN THOMAS

< Mousehole from the Air

Mousehole Dawn >

September 8, 1810.- Before breakfast made a finished sketch of St. Michael's Mount from the Star Inn. I next hired a boat with two fisherman to take me round the island, which they undertook to do and to allow me time for making sketches, for a reward of four shillings. The weather was very fine, and the sea sufficiently smooth to enable them to keep the boat nearly stationary wherever I chose to remain.

JOSEPH FARINGTON

Penzance >

< St. Michael's Mount

TRENARREN : AUTUMN 1941

The thunder-green sea
Brings nearer the Island
On which stood the chapel
Of Michael the Archangel.

Smoke from a chimney
In the V-shaped valley,
The voices of children,
A robin on the bough:

Familiar and cheerful
Domestic noises
Speak of contentment
About me now.

But what is to come?
I ask myself, waiting
In this burial-place
Of my ancient people:

The long-headed, dark-faced
Mediterranean
Men who drove prows
Into these inlets:

Confronting the danger
That they too awaited
In the urgent whisper,
The winter sea waiting.

A L ROWSE

The cry of 'heva' was echoed all around by those working in the fields who would at once throw down spade or pick or whatever implement was in their hands and rush helter-skelter down to launch the boats and cast the net before the shoal moved out of Gunwalloe's territorial waters. An oar stuck up on the beach of Church Cove halfway between Church Cove and the Poldhu cliffs marked the boundary. Beyond that the territorial waters of the Gunwalloe Daws became those of the Mullion Gulls, and many a fight had there been in the past over the position of a shoal and the right to net it.

SIR COMPTON MACKENZIE

Today by force of elemental passion nature has opened her own paint box. See her sweep across the landscape a blue black storm! Now watch her efface that darkness with a brushful of gold. Of colour multifarious is this frame to Mount's Bay whose turbulent waters mirror the sky.

DAME LAURA KNIGHT

< Mullion Island

Gunwalloe Church Cove >

*T*hen comes the sudden swirl round of the wind, the blustering gale from the south-west, the dragging anchor, the lee shore, and last battle in the creaming breakers. The wise mariner stands far out from that evil place.

SIR ARTHUR CONAN DOYLE

< Winter Gale

Mullion Harbour >

*O*n the Monday and Tuesday at Redruth there was such a storm as had not been known for thirty-five years in West Cornwall. It, snowed almost incessantly for twenty-four hours, and left drifts, in some parts, from ten to twelve feet deep. The trains could not get into Redruth either from the east or west for two days, and even Camborne could not be reached. .... Milk could hardly be obtained, and what butter was in the market was sold at the price of 2s.per lb., a heavy price for Redruth. There was a scarcity of coals in the neighbourhood, and the stock (of coals) at the brewery was exhausted before the end of the week.

ANON

< Cornish Winter

Snow on The Lizard Coast >

It was a singular spot, and one peculiarly well suited to the grim humour of my patient. From the windows of our little white-washed house, which stood high upon a grassy headland, we looked down upon the whole sinister semi-circle of Mounts Bay, that old death trap of sailing vessels, with its fringe of black cliffs and surge-swept reefs on which innumerable seamen have met their end. With a northerly breeze it lies placid and sheltered, inviting the storm tossed craft to tack into it for rest and protection.

SIR ARTHUR CONAN DOYLE

Prinsep and I each began a drawing of Asparagus Island, and as we settled to work, Tennyson proved how, despite his short-sightedness, he had acquired the knowledge of details found in his poems.

HOLMAN HUNT

Kynance Sunset >

< Winter Sea

THE EAGLE

He clasps the crag with hooked hands;
Close to the sun in lonely lands,
Ring'd with the azure world, he stands.

The wrinkled sea beneath him crawls;
He watches from his mountain walls,
And like a thunderbolt he falls.

ALFRED LORD TENNYSON

Now, what magic spell is shed,
Like a dream the years had sped;
Dream-like, gone the fears and frets,
Gone the longings and regrets;
Your glad ray at last requites
All our sorrow, Lizard Lights!.

KENNETH GRAHAME

*T*he full moon was waiting to greet us at Minack, a soft breeze came from the sea and the Lizard light winked every few seconds across Mount's Bay. An owl hooted in the wood and afar off I heard the wheezing bark, like a hyena, of a vixen. A fishing boat chugged by, a mile off shore, its starboard light bright on the mast. It was very still. The boulders, so massive in the day, had become gossamer in the moonlight, and the cottage, so squat and solid, seemed to be floating in the centuries of its past.

DEREK TANGYE

< Goonhilly Earth Station

The Lizard Lighthouse >

52

*W*ere Cadgwith a little nearer civilisation, what a show-place it would become!

DINAH MULOCH CRAIK

The last is situated near Cadgwith. a small fishing village sheltered by steep hills, possessing what the English call a romantic character. Here I hired a boat; the sea was perfectly calm, and no boatman of Cadgwith would venture near this dangerous coast in dubious weather. We first visited the Frying-pan, which, seen from the coast, certainly offers grand features; in the dark mass of rocks opens an arch, into which the light of days pours, and under which aquatic birds fly.

ALPHONSE ESQUIROS

It is proposed to go some to some hole in Cornwall named Cadgwith, to sea-bathe my weak ankle.

I miss you, as you would be happy here, and I like to be with you when you are happy.

Coast Path >

< Cadgwith

GEORGE BERNARD SHAW

55

Rhythms of lonely Constantine - the arc
Of the wide bay, the billowy dunes, the long
Atlantic roll.

To look on the translucent green, the blue
Deepening to purple where the weed is dense!
To hear the homing call as the brave sweep
Of wings is folded on a sea-girt rock!
To lie in golden warmth, while tow'ring waves
Break with a lazy roar along the beach
To lie and dream.

A perfect dream! That I
Might sleep for ever by the ruined church
Whose threshold is the sacrificial stone
Of a forgotten people, if such dream
Were mine.

C J GLAISHER

The long rollers of the Channel, travelling from beyond Lizard point,
follow hard upon the steep seas at the river mouth, and mingling with
the surge and wash of deep sea water comes the brown tide, swollen
with the last rains and brackish from the mud, bearing upon its face
dead twigs and straws, and strange forgotten things, leaves too early
fallen, young birds, and the buds of flowers. The open roadstead is
deserted, for an east wind makes uneasy anchorage, and but for the few
houses scattered here and there above Helford passage, and the group of
bungalows about Port Navas, the river would be the same as it was in
a century now forgotten, in a time that has left few memories.

DAPHNE DU MAURIER

Cornish Cottage >

< Gillan Creek

The sea sweeps into a magnificent harbour, and off the harbour run broad arms of water - now blue, now green - that feel their way deep into the recesses of the hills; and themselves in many cases throw off other arms that go in countless ramifications through the countryside. All are subject to the sea, so that the surge and sigh of waters governed by the steadfast laws of the tides draw music through all the hollows of the hills. Great ships go up and anchor deep in the heart of the country; and at every turning one may come upon an inland village with a sweep of shingle beach, a tiny jetty, and a marine flavour.

HOWARD SPRING

I have blundered into a Garden of Eden that cannot be described in pen or paint.

H V MORTON

< *Helston Flora*

Helford Dawn >

*Y*ou can only see Cornwall or know anything about it by
walking through it - it is romantic to a degree, though probably
one would not like to live in it.

GEORGE BORROW

*W*oke & forgot all my travelling troubles after a long sweet
sleep. & found myself in a very charming house, in a pretty
room & with a pleasant family…….

WILLIAM MAKEPEACE THACKERAY

Estuary Sunrise >

< Falmouth

This town of Falmouth, as you will partly conjecture, is no great ways from the sea. It is defended on the sea-side by twin castles, St.Mawes and Pendennis, extremely well calculated for annoying every body except an enemy. St.Mawes is garrisoned by an ablebodied person of fourscore, a widower. He has the whole command and sole management of six most unmanageable pieces of ordnance, admirably adapted for destruction of Pendennis, a like tower of strength on the opposite side of the Channel.

LORD BYRON

Truro >

< St. Mawes Castle

The day we passed through Falmouth, that last village was Portloe. Charming, I noted in my diary later, noting also that, as had happened with the sky, the search for adjectives to suitably describe fishing villages was putting a strain on my vocabulary: delightful, cute, enchanting, idyllic, picturesque, exquisite, nice, I'd used them all. I decided to adapt the Beaufort Scale of wind speeds and apply it to charm. Twelve different levels, registering ferocity, of enchantment.

MARK WALLINGTON

I reached the top of the cliffs and paused for a moment to look down on the calm leaden sea that heaved gently against the rock-bound coast. The cry of the gulls was balm to the turmoil of my thoughts. That high screaming cry had always been synonymous with holidays to me, for from my earliest childhood I had always spent them on rocky coastland. There was peace here and quiet. I looked back at the little group of cottages huddling down the valley to the cove. It was satisfying to think that whatever happened this coast and the cottage would remain to bring peace of mind to those who lived on and to other generations.

HAMMOND INNES

< Bodinnick

St. Just in Roseland >

There lay spread, not one of your dainty afternoon teas, with two or three wafery slices of bread and butter, but a regular substantial meal. Cheerful candles - of course in serpentine candlesticks - were already lit, and showed us a bright teapot full of that welcome drink to weary travellers, hot, strong and harmless; the gigantic home-baked loaf, which it seemed sacrilegious to have turned into toast; the rich, yellow butter - I am sure those lovely cows had something to do with it, and also with the cream, so thick that the spoon could almost have stood upright in it. Besides, there was a quantity of that delicious clotted cream, which here accompanies every meal and of which I had vainly tried to get the receipt, but was answered with polite scorn, "Oh, ma'am, it would be of no use to you: Cornish cream can only be made from Cornish cows!"

DINAH MULOCH CRAIK

< Pub Sign

Portloe >

*A*nd talking of seagulls, I was about to enter Seagull City, otherwise known as Mevagissey. Here the birds swooped down the alleyways in squadrons like something Barnes Wallis had designed, dropping their bombs with a white splat on the pavement. Fortunately, these didn't bounce, but in a place like this, it was only a matter of time before one was hit.

MARK WALLINGTON

One needs to come to Cornwall to
believe in the amount of colouring
which is possible about boats.

BEATRIX POTTER

Of all views I reckon that of a harbour the most fascinating and the most easeful, for it combines perpetual change with perpetual repose. It amuses like a panorama and soothes like an opiate, and when you have realised this you will understand why so many thousands of men around this island appear to spend all their time in watching tidal water. Lest you should suspect me of taking a merely dilettante interest in the view, I must add that I am a Harbour Commissioner.

SIR ARTHUR QUILLER COUCH 'Q'

< Charlestown

Fowey Sunset >

It was so very beautiful that the Mole could only hold up both fore paws and gasp, "O my! O my! O my!"

KENNETH GRAHAME

The romance of Cornwall has once again overcome me. I find lapses into a particular mood of absolute enjoyment which takes me back into my childhood.

VIRGINIA WOOLF

Lerryn Reflections >

< Lerryn

Come all good Cornish boys walk in,

Here's brandy, rum, and shrub, and gin;

You can't do less than drink success

To copper, fish, and tin.

ANON

Except in thick mist or in high summer I hardly remember still air at Gorran. The wind either played or howled round our house; it rarely died altogether. It was a constant companion, in one's hair and in the leaves and in the telegraph poles, whirling the smoke down the chimneys, rattling the sash windows, and bringing the middle door to with a bang if front or back were suddenly opened. When I was told the story of Jacob wrestling with God I saw him struggling to open our heavy front door in the wind.

ANN TRENEER

<Fishing Nets

Lobster Pots>

*P*olperro was a village of whitewashed cottages tumbled together in a rocky ravine on the sea. The streets were as narrow as alleys and few of them could take motor vehicles. I saw a full-sized bus try to make it down one street hopeless. At best, one small car could inch down a street knocking petals off geraniums in the window boxes at either side. When two cars met head-on there was usually an argument over who was to reverse to let the other pass.

PAUL THEROUX

Polperrow is a small fishing port almost wholly inhabited by fishermen…. Everything that comes into view has a character of simplicity, and is in perfect unison. It is formed for the Landscape Painter.

JOSEPH FARRINGTON

Gull on Boat >

< Polperro

*C*ornwall is not like any other sort of country - it's no use trying to compare it with any other place. There are times when you feel you are not properly you, but someone else whom you don't in the least bit know; and an atmosphere prevails which takes away any sense or belief you have ever had, and you don't know why, but you aren't in England any more.

DAME LAURA KNIGHT

There is a strangeness about Cornwall. You feel it as soon as you cross Tor Ferry.

H V MORTON

Banjo Pier, Looe >

< Looe Fishing Boat at Dawn

If a man dreamt of a great pile of stones in a nightmare, he would dream of such a pile as the Cheese-Wring. All the heaviest and largest of the seven thick slabs of which it is composed are at the top; all the lightest and smallest at the bottom. It rises perpendicularly to a height of thirty-two feet, without lateral support of any kind. The fifth and sixth rocks are of immense size and thickness, and overhang fearfully, all round, the forth lower rocks support them. All are perfectly irregular; the projections of one do not fit into the interstices of another; they are heaped up loosely in their extraordinary top-heavy form, on slanting ground half-way down a steep hill. Look at them from whatever point you choose, there is still all that is heaviest, largest, strongest, at the summit, and all that is lightest, smallest, weakest, at the base. When you first see the Cheese-Wring, you instinctively shrink from walking under it. Beholding the tons on tons of stone balanced to a hair's breadth on the mere fragments beneath, you think that with a pole in your hand, with on push against the top rocks you could hurl down the hill in an instant a pile which has stood for centuries, unshaken by the fiercest hurricane that ever blew, rushing from the great void of an ocean over the naked surface of a moor.

WILKIE COLLINS

A thrill came over me as I surveyed this gigantic erection. I climbed to the top of the stone, put my arm through the hole and shouted "Success to Old Cornwall!"

GEORGE BORROW

Trevethy Quoit >

< The Cheesewring

*O*ur mists were mostly in rapid motion, borne on breezes or even whirled on gales. They poured across the downs in a wild and eddying torrent, as if the sea had been drained of its vapours to overwhelm the land. But every now and then, in fair calm weather, surface fog would collect in the hollows of the moor. Sometimes, when riding home at night, I have seen the upper slopes of our fields, crowned by the tall trees in the yard, stand sharp and clear against a host of stars, while the shallow dell at the bridge beyond was full of mist that lay at peace like standing water, faintly bright in the gleam of distant worlds; so that the place had the look of a peat-moss in Uist, where there is more loch than land.

MARGARET LEIGH

Moorland Sheep >

< Bodmin Moor and Roughtor

It is very lovely here. I am sitting with my back against a boulder, a few yards above the houses. Below, the gorse is yellow, and the sea is blue. It is very still, no sound but the birds and the wind among the stones. A very big seagull just flew up from the east, white like lime-stone, and hovered just in front of me, then turned back in the sky. It seemed like a messenger.

D H LAWRENCE

When your reach the head of the Valley it is as if you came suddenly on sunshine rising from the soil. The three slopes enclose you with light and colour and fragrance, for the gorse is all abloom. You drink in the scent and the brilliance and the colour of it till you are conscious of nothing else and your whole being is just a clear gold flame.

C C VYVYAN

Golitha Falls >

< Bodmin Moor

What makes a landscape? Obviously the natural topography the hills or plains, coasts or moors, rivers or estuaries is involved. This provides the underlying framework. But landscape is not just a matter of physical geography. It's also the result of centuries of human toil. What many see as "natural" is in fact man and woman made. The fields, the hedges, the woods, the very bumps and dips in the surface are the result of the sweat and effort of generations of Cornish people. Landscape is also community. It is the visible link between us and our past.

COSERG

China Clay Tips >

< Cornish Hedge

*F*rom Saltash to St Germans, Liskeard and St Austell,
The County of Cornwall was all in a bustle,
Prince Albert is coming the people did say
To open the Bridge and the Cornish Railway.
From Redruth, and Camborne, St Just in the west
The people did flock all dressed in their best.
From all parts of England you'll now have a chance
To travel by steam right down to Penzance.

ANON

A bitter moment it was when the Tamar was crossed and Cornwall
left behind, perhaps for ever. I seemed to linger once more over the last
fond look at the Cornish sea. And in what company. I thought -
was it so - that there were tears in those blue eyes when we parted. I
know there were tears in mine. Forget me not, oh, forget me not.

FRANCIS KILVERT

< Brunel's Tamar Bridge

89

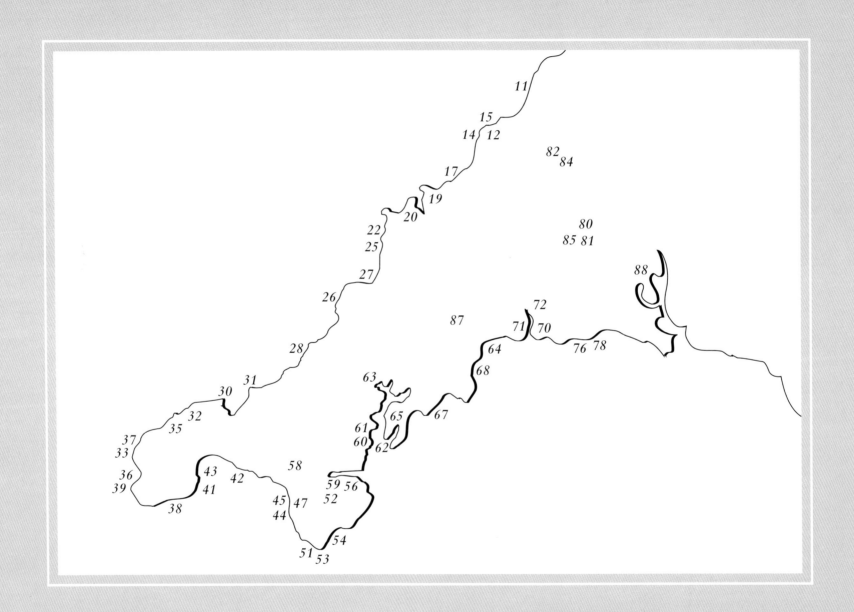

INDEX

The index includes fuller captions to the photographs in page order.

The National Trust owns many properties in Cornwall, especially on the coast. When substantial amounts of Trust property are included in a photograph the entries have been indicated with a star.

Once upon a time there were two Cornish Giants. One lived on St.Michael's Mount while his friend lived on the mainland. So close were they that they shared a giant hammer. One day the Giant on the Mount called to his friend to throw him the hammer. Just at that moment his wife came out of her home. She was struck dead by the hammer as it flew through the air. Although greatly grieved the Giant lifted up the Mount and tucked her underneath. To this day if you look down the well on St. Michael's Mount you can see her eye looking up at you!

43 PENZANCE

At the end of the railway line, Penzance is a centre for exploring western Cornwall. With Newlyn just along the promenade attracting artists in the last century the town has kept a lively ambience.

44 MULLION ISLAND ★

Spring flowers create a necklace of colour along the edge of the cliffs in May. The island is a bird sanctuary.

45 GUNWALLOE ★

The sandy cove at Gunwalloe has a church at one end sheltered in the lee of the cliffs.

46 WINTER GALE

The sea is turned into a turbulent cauldron of seething water when westerly gales sweep in from the Atlantic.

47 MULLION HARBOUR STORM ★

The harbour wall at Mullion was built in 1895 to protect this tiny cove from winter gales. I have witnessed a huge wave which completely covered both arms of the harbour.

48 WINTER LANDSCAPE

Snow is rare in Cornwall. The lack of trees in the south-west is due to high winds rather than blizzards.

49 SNOW ON CLIFFS ★

When snow arrives the cliffside is transformed into a wonderland.

50 WINTER SEA

The contrast of summer and winter is noticed by the mood of the sea.

51 KYNANCE ★

Kynance has long been a favourite spot with visitors. A sandy beach, caves, a blow hole and spectacular cliffside views unfortunately lead to excessive erosion.

52 GOONHILLY DISHES

Famed for the first Telstar link across the atlantic the British Telecom Earth Station at Goonhilly celebrated 25 years of T.V. and telephone communications in 1987.

53 LIZARD LIGHTHOUSE

The Lizard is Britain's most southerly point. Cornwall's first lighthouse was built here in 1619. This photograph was taken very near to the spot where the Spanish Armada was first sighted in 1588. During the quadricentennial celebrations the mist was so thick that even the sea could not be seen. If the same weather had happened 400 years earlier we would all be speaking Spanish!

54 CADGWITH

Probably the most picturesque of all Cornish fishing coves. The boats winched up onto the shingle beach are nearly all commercial fishing boats.

55 COAST PATH ★

Sea Pinks, or Thrift, line the coast path just north of Cadgwith.

56 GILLAN CREEK ★

The easterly side of the Lizard Peninsula shows a more gentle, sheltered face than the western coast, which faces the full force of winter gales.

57 COTTAGE

58 HELSTON FLORA

Each May 8th the Furry or Floral Dance is

danced in the streets of Helson. Although in its present form the dance dates from early Victorian times a similar ritual is believed to have taken place before christianity.

59 HELFORD MISTY DAWN

This small village on the Helford estuary has a completely different character to the western side of the Lizard peninsula. In narrow sheltered creeks the landscape is calmer and more gentle. The estuary here is a natural oysterage and is also popular with sailors.

60 FALMOUTH

Falmouth has one of the best natural harbours in Europe. It is little used except for the ships arriving and leaving the repair docks. In the days of sail the Falmouth Packet boats were an important part of maritime communications. During the time of emigration from Cornwall to the United States, the fare to London by stagecoach, was more than the fare to America from Falmouth.

61 ESTUARY DAWN

The Fal estuary is a favourite spot for boats of all sizes.

62 ST MAWES CASTLE

Guarding the approach to the Carrick Roads the castle was built in 1540. It surrendered to Cromwell's forces during the Civil War as the castle guns could only point towards the sea.

63 TRURO

The cathedral which made Truro the unofficial capital of Cornwall was built between 1880 and 1910. The terrace of georgian houses in the foreground are much older.

64 BODINNICK

A tiny hamlet facing Fowey across the estuary. Most visitors pass by. Daphne du Maurier lived here in a house first bought by her father.

65 ST JUST IN ROSELAND

There is an enchanting story that Joseph of Arimathea, who was a tin merchant, brought Jesus Christ here while a boy. Whether he left behind the seeds of the many sub-tropical plants which grow in the churchyard is not mentioned.

66 PUB SIGN ★

The brewery companies are destroying many traditional pubs with inappropriate modernisation. However, there are still a few left. If you are lucky, apart from good beer, you may hear an impromptu sing-song of Cornish fisherman.

67 PORTLOE

One of Cornwall's smaller but most charming villages.

68 & 69 MEVAGISSEY

From small beginnings in the middle ages, the fishing port of Mevagissey grew much larger in the 18th and 19th centuries, from the catching of pilchards.

70 CHARLESTOWN

Built by Charles Rashleigh at the end of the 18th century the port was designed by John Smeaton, builder of the famous Eddystone lighthouse.

71 FOWEY SUNSET

A wide estuary separates the town of Fowey from Polruan on the opposite bank. The waters are a centre for sailing, while up-river the wharves of the china clay industry bring bigger ships.

72 & 73 LERRYN

The indented estuaries of South Cornwall provide sheltered anchorage for boats of all types. Lerryn is typical of many other quiet backwaters.

74 & 75 FISHING GEAR

Rope and Pots, the tools of fishing, are found in all Cornwall's fishing coves and are a reminder of an age old traditional industry.

76 & 77 POLPERRO

Probably the most famous of Cornwall's fishing villages Polperro has been a mecca to artists and writers for many years. Crowded in mid-summer it reverts, in winter, to a peaceful place, where commercial fishing boats jostle for space on the tiny quays.

78 & 79 LOOE

New buildings for the fish market have helped Looe become a rival fishing centre to Plymouth and Newlyn. However it still retains a holiday aspect with a beach sheltered by the distinctive Banjo Pier.

80 THE CHEESEWRING

Although considered by many to be part of the megalithic landscape of Cornwall the Cheesewring is a natural feature. The peculiar stacking of the rocks occurred over millions of years of erosion.

81 TREVETHY QUOIT

This megalithic monument on the edge of Bodmin Moor has a famous hole in the topmost stone.

82 BODMIN MOOR & ROUGHTOR

Cornwall's high moor of Bodmin is a bleak and desolate place in winter.

83 MOORLAND SHEEP ★

Hardy sheep graze on the moors. The stone hedges provide ideal shelter from cold winds.

84 BODMIN MOOR

Away from the exposed hilltops parts of the moor are soft and gentle.

85 GOLITHA FALLS

Waters from Bodmin Moor tumble down to the sea in many streams and rivers. Here the upper reaches of the river Fowey plunge through a series of cascades.

86 CORNISH HEDGE

In parts of West Penwith, and Bodmin Moor, the traditional stone hedges were made from the rocks found when the area was cleared for fields. In other areas the stone was imported from a local quarry. The quarries were often owned by the hedge builders and their style of wall depended on the stone available. In this way many different styles developed. This wall in North Cornwall is in the 'Jack and Jill' pattern.

87 CLAY TIPS

When pottery clay was first discovered here, it was at the height of the boom in imported ware from China. All of the English potteries were desperate to obtain supplies of finer clay to match the chinese quality. The St. Austell area became their salvation and soon Wedgwood, Doulton, Royal Worcester and others were able to compete with the chinese. The distinctive lunar landscape are the tips of waste material after the clay has been washed out.

88 BRUNEL'S BRIDGE

Built for the Great Western Railway Company by Isambard Kingdom Brunel the bridge across the Tamar into Devon is a potent symbol of the gap between Cornwall and the rest of the country.

THE WRITERS

SVEN BERLIN
JOHN BETJEMAN
GEORGE BORROW
WILLIAM BORROW
SIR JAMES BROOKE
LORD BYRON
CHARLES CAUSLEY
WILKIE COLLINS
MARGARET ANN COURTNEY
NOEL COWARD
FREDERICK COWLS
C A DAWSON
CHARLES DICKENS
SIR ARTHUR CONAN DOYLE
DAPHNE DU MAURIER
ALPHONSE ESQUIROS
W Y EVANS WENTZ
JOSEPH FARINGTON
NORMAN GARSTIN
DAVIS GILBERT
KENNETH GRAHAME
THOMAS HARDY
J HARRIS STONE
ROBERT STEPHEN HAWKER
HENRY HAWKINS
CHARLES HENDERSON
HOLMAN HUNT
HAMMOND INNES
ROBERT FRANCIS KILVERT
DAME LAURA KNIGHT
D H LAWRENCE
MARGARET LEIGH
JOHN LELAND
LONGFELLOW
SIR COMPTON MACKENZIE
H V MORTON
DINAH MULOCK CRAIK
BEATRIX POTTER
HENRY QUICK
SIR ARTHUR QUILLER-COUCH
A L ROWSE
WILLIAM SHAKESPEARE

GEORGE BERNARD SHAW
HOWARD SPRING
ALGERNON SWINBURNE
ARTHUR SYMONS
DEREK TANGYE
ALFRED LORD TENNYSON
THAKERAY
PAUL THEROUX
ANNE TRENEER
DENYS VAL BAKER
C C VYVYAN
PETER WARLOCK
VIRGINIA WOOLF

PHOTOGRAPHER'S NOTES

Photography is like fishing. You go out in the morning with no idea of what the trip will bring. Sometimes luck is on your side and all your crab pots are full of prime Lobsters. Other times you get nothing.

Of course I tip the scales in my favour by researching everything from tide times to weather conditions. I also check if scaffolding has been removed from prominent buildings.

I use a very ordinary camera just like many amateurs. There are no fancy creative techniques which some cameras do and others do not. They all require the same creative eye to get good results.

It is usual in books of photographs like this for the photographer to have a page describing his or her techniques and equipment. In this instance those who like to know of lenses, film, f/stops and such will have to do without. Technique is a matter of individual preferences. It bores me. I am only interested in results. However I do offer a few guiding rules of photography.

1/ My essential equipment includes an alarm clock to wake up early and a compass to find where the sun is going to be. I also have a small double pointed quartz crystal which sits in my camera bag with the exposed film and helps to increase sharpness!

2/ The best light occurs when I am stuck in the office with the VAT man or have left my camera at home.

3/ If I wait for perfect conditions someone will park a truck in the view.

4/ The most I have waited in the rain for conditions to improve was five days. The picture wasn't worth waiting for and isn't in this book.

5/ Having walked for miles for a good picture I often find the best photo when I return is right next to my car. The only problem being that I've parked right in the middle of the view.

6/ Nothing is repeatable especially the light.

7/ Those pictures which require the most perspiration and imagination to take are always the ones that look the easiest.

8/ Don't run out of film.

Some of these photographs were taken for the "Atmosphere" range of postcards which I launched ten years ago. The collection has been added to every year. From the outset I attempted to show what others shied away from. My first range of postcards had no blue sky in any of the photographs. To be original is difficult. It is even harder to be original and remain true to popular perceptions. I hope I have succeeded.

'Our stay at this delightful hamlet was slightly unhappily cut short by our stock of dry plates becoming exhausted, so that beyond a visit to the giant headland of Castle Treryn, and the Logan rock, there was no alternative but to return to headquarters (Penzance), and replenish before resuming our pilgrimage.'

HENRY HAWKINS 1904

Also remember Norman Garstin's adage:

'Your work cannot really be good unless you have caught a cold doing it'

ACKNOWLEDGEMENTS

Special thanks to Julie for all her help without which this book would not be ready till next year. Also I would like to thank Bill and Sue.

Thanks to A L Rowse for kindly allowing me to use valuable research from his book "A Cornish Anthology". His encouragement was the impetus which started the collection of quotes in this book. His poem "Trenarren:Autumn 1941" appears on page 43. Other valuable sources were "A View From Land's End" and "A Literary Landscape" by Denys Val Baker. Thanks to Martin for pointing me in that direction. Thanks also to Ian Martin for helping me with research which was first published in "Literary Trails".

Many thanks to Ann Butcher for the stylish design.
Also thanks to Dave at Scantec.

The quotations from THE TIMELESS LAND & A WORK OF ART by Denys Val Baker are reproduced with permission of Jess Val Baker.
The quotation from BRITAIN'S ART COLONY BY THE SEA by Sven Berlin is reproduced with permission of Sven Berlin.
The quotations from the work of George Bernard Shaw and the quotation from MY LIFE AND TIMES by Sir Compton Mackenzie are reproduced with kind permission of The Society of Authors.
The quotation from WRECKERS MUST BREATHE by Hammond Innes is reproduced with permission of Curtis Brown Ltd, London on behalf of Hammond Innes. Copyright 1940 by Hammond Innes.
The quotation from THE KINGDOM OF THE SEA by Paul Theroux is reproduced with permission of Hamish Hamilton Ltd. Copyright 1983 by Paul Theroux.
The quotations from IN SEARCH OF ENGLAND(1927) by H.V.Morton are reproduced with permission of Methuen London Ltd
The quotation from COLLECTED POEMS by Charles Causley is reproduced with permission of David Higham Associates.
The quotation from COLLECTED POEMS by John Betjeman is reproduced with permission of John Murray Ltd.
The quotation from the Autobiography of Noel Coward is reproduced with permission of Michael Imison Playwrights Ltd.
The quotations from 500 MILE WALKIES by Mark Wallington are reproduced with permission of Hutchinson Publishers.
The quotations from CORNISH SILHOUETTES by C.C.Vyvyan are reproduced with permission of Barbara Fox.
The quotation from SCHOOL HOUSE IN THE WIND by Anne Treneer is reproduced with permission of Bodley Head.
The quotation from A GULL ON THE ROOF by Derek Tangye is reproduced with permission of Michael Joseph Ltd. Copyright Derek Tangye 1986.
The quotations from THE JOURNAL OF BEATRIX POTTER by Beatrix Potter are reproduced with permission of Frederick Warne.
The quotation from A CORNISH WINDOW by Sir Arthur Quiller-Couch is reproduced with permission of Cambridge University Press.
The quotations from THE MAGIC OF A LINE by Dame Laura Knight are reproduced with permission of John Farquharson Ltd. London.
The quotation from CORNWALL AT THE CROSSROADS by CoSerg is reproduced with kind permission of the authors.
The quotation from WINDS OF THE DAY by Howard Spring is reproduced with permission of Harper Collins Publishers Ltd.
The quotation from FRENCHMAN'S CREEK by Daphne Du Maurier is reproduced with permission of Curtis Brown Ltd. London on behalf of The Chichester Partnership.
The quotation from The Collected Letters (1912 - 1922) of Virginia Woolf is reproduced with permission of The Hogarth Press.

Every effort has been made to contact all copyright-holders. Should the publishers have made any mistakes in attribution we will be pleased to make the necessary arrangements at the first opportunity.